You Too Can Be A Democratic Candidate For President

Other Books By the Authors:

The Rites of Spring: A Student's Guide
To Spring Break in Florida

Europe: Where the Fun Is

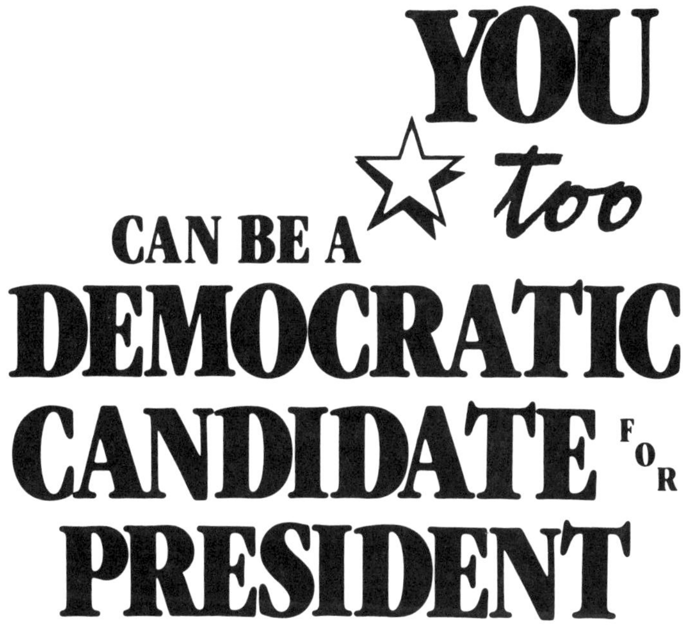

BRUCE JACOBSEN
ROLLIN RIGGS

Kampmann Publishing/RJ Publications
New York/New Haven

Library of Congress Catalog Number: 83-82916

ISBN: 0-914457-02-0

10 9 8 7 6 5 4 3 2

Cover design by Deborah Daley.
Interior design by Rollin Riggs.

PICTURE CREDITS: pg. 40, UPI; pg. 45, Los Angeles Times; pg. 47, Rollin Riggs; pg. 50, Rollin Riggs; pg. 77, NBC.

*This book is dedicated to Harold Stassen.
Although a Republican, Mr. Stassen has been
a candidate for President twelve times,
and he's still going strong.
He is an inspiration to us all.*

Table of Contents

Acknowledgements

Our sincere thanks to Bruce Shaw, Court Chilton, John Glenn, Debbie Mercer, Robert Scannell, Eric M. Kampmann, Ramsay and Edye MacMullen, Julie Williams, the Democratic Party (what a party!), Caitlin Doyle, Walter Mondale, Joy Harris, Betsy Cavendish, Jesse Jackson, Sam Freedman, Al Cranston, Nancy and Richard Sayford, Reubin Askew, Bruce Shaw again, Gary Hart, Smiley at Perkins, Fritz Hollings, Michael Natan, Michael Shavelson, George McGovern for making us feel young again, the cast of The Love Boat, Brooke Shields, the Federal Election Commission, Carol Theodore, Emily Buss and Betsy Bradley, the Oyster Bar (despite its prices), New Balance running shoes, Howard Brown and his extended family, Jennifer Beals, Ronald Reagan for making all of this possible, and, of course, our parents — Arthur and Elizabeth Jacobsen, and Webster and Sandy Riggs — for their contributions to the RJP PAC.

Bruce Jacobsen
Rollin Riggs

December, 1983

Introduction

Don't be intimidated by the idea of running for President — people of a lot less quality than you have done it. The last two Presidents were a peanut farmer and an actor, and one of the strongest contenders this time is an astronaut, so obviously no particular background is required. Anyway, you have lots of skills: if Florida Governor Bob Graham can qualify for his post by working for a day at jobs like a garbageman or telephone repairman, think how many skills you've acquired by being a garbageman all your life. Obviously, you're Presidential material.

Don't worry about the issues, either. There are just too many of them out there to keep straight, and besides, who believes what politicians say? Issues don't divide the candidates: images do. No one can remember the differences between Jerry Ford and Jimmy Carter: both were for a strong defense, both were against waste in government, both were for more jobs. Quick, name their differences on the Social Security issue. You see? The difference was images: Jimmy Carter's stupid smile, Jerry Ford's inability to walk down the stairs of the airplane. We remember Jimmy because of his brother Billy, and Jerry for playing too much football without a helmet. In this book we will deal with the real issues — the images.

Don't worry about money, either: you can sell out for a high price. Just get that ball rolling, and the oil people and the doctors' lobby will come running. Politics these days is designed for dark horses like you. All you have to do is win in New Hampshire, a state whose biggest city has only 87,000 residents. One respectable showing and the Ivy League interns and high-priced lawyers will start banging on your door. And federal equal time requirements force the media to give you attention.

Concentrate on the benefits of the job: $200,000 a year, good seats at the Redskins games, meeting Jane Pauley, being able to nuke Iran if they act up again, yelling at

Jesse Helms. Think how much **you** could make of the position: getting Bruce Springsteen to sing the national anthem at your inaugaration, giving away free beer instead of free cheese, making Tom Selleck or Brooke Shields your National Security Adviser.

Just as important, think about being an ex-President: selling your memoirs for $2 million, lecturing at $15,000 a shot, and playing golf with Bob Hope. According to *Time* magazine, the government spends $26 million a year just taking care of former Presidents. With no effort at all, you could double that figure.

This book should help you understand what presidential politics today really involves, and we'll try to get you started on the right foot. We've supplied nearly everything you need to become a Democratic candidate for President — addresses of the biggest political action committees, sample press releases, photos, great advice, and much more.

Finally, if all goes according to plan and you do end up taking the Oath of Office, just remember who helped you get the keys to 1600 Pennsylvania Avenue — we did, Bruce Jacobsen and Rollin Riggs. First, you'll need someone to help you work on your memoirs. We're available, and our agent will contact you. We'll even help you negotiate an advance with a publisher. Second, when it's time choose a new ambassador to Tahiti, well, you have our address.

Of course, if you choose to forget the guys that made it all possible, that would signal to us that you don't want to be a two-term President. In other words, if we don't hear from you real soon after the election, we'll start to work on our next book: *You Too Can Be a Republican Candidate for President.*

Test Your Qualifications

Do you have the right stuff to be President? Answer this 20-question quiz to find out.

1. You want to be President because

    a) you want to bring peace and prosperity to the planet.

    b) if Jerry Ford and Jimmy Carter can do it, why can't I?

    c) it beats driving a truck.

    d) a $200,000 a year salary, $150,000 a year for expenses, a one million dollar transition fund...

2. If elected you promise

    a) to do your utmost to fulfill your campaign promises.

    b) not to run for re-election.

    c) to investigate the problems of beach erosion in Tahiti.

    d) never to pre-empt *The Love Boat*.

3. When a reporter uncovers the illegal $500,000 donation you got from the Teamsters, you will

    a) deny knowledge of it and order an unbiased investigation.

    b) offer him 10 percent.

    c) blame it on a computer error.

    d) defend it as a legitimate political statement from America's working class.

    e) consider question #7.

4. The prime quality of a President is

  a) humanity, intellect, and understanding.
  b) large contributions and little intelligence.
  c) a good golf game.
  d) actually wanting the job.

5. Politics means

  a) never having to work for a living.
  b) you didn't make partner.
  c) valuing your friends very highly ($1,000 a
     plate).
  d) getting your name in the paper.

6. Executive privilege means

  a) never having to say your sorry.
  b) ignoring the courts, Congress and your spouse.
  c) getting to call Jesse Helms any name you want.
  d) getting good seats at the theater.

**7. What is the first thing that comes to mind when
you hear the word "prison?"**

  a) My vice president can pardon me.
  b) Where did I get that dog, anyway?
  c) Those deductions on the '81 returns.
  d) Junior, again.

8. The Washington Redskins' best play is

  a) Riggins off tackle.
  b) signing Riggins.
  c) scheduling the Baltimore Colts.
  d) not arguing with Riggins, whatever he wants.

9. Congress is

  a) the representative of the American people.
  b) only a little less crooked than the President.
  c) a new punk rock group from Australia.
  d) the opposite of Progress.

10. You want to be remembered

   a) as the President who made the country great
   b) more than Jerry Ford.
   c) more than your alcoholic brother.
   d) in the dairy farmers' political contributions.

11. The prime attribute of a Vice President is

   a) being a "team player."
   b) the ability to mix a good martini.
   c) coming from the opposite end of the country.
   d) lack of ambition.

12. The best President in the last century was

   a) Franklin D. Roosevelt.
   b) Calvin Coolidge.
   c) Ronald Reagan.
   d) Nancy Reagan.

13. In debates, always question your opponent's

   a) voting record.
   b) 1981 tax returns.
   c) taste in clothes.
   d) sexual proclivities.

14. Your slogan will be

   a) "Peace and prosperity for all."
   b) "Vote for me."
   c) "Please vote for me."
   d) "Really, you won't be sorry."

**15. When an opponent questions your integrity,
you**

   a) question his.
   b) say "I'm rubber and you're glue. Everything
      you say bounces off me and sticks to you."
   c) call it McCarthyism.
   d) mention your childhood poverty, your rank as
      an Eagle Scout, and the death of your mother

16. You're the "little person's candidate" because

    a) you believe the bureaucracy often ignores the average American.
    b) the oil company PAC's were committed.
    c) all the other minorities were committed.
    d) they vote.

17. Your favorite reading material is

    a) the Washington *Post* and the New York *Times*.
    b) your opponent's briefing book.
    c) *Highlights*.
    d) Cliff Notes.

18. Your "Kitchen Cabinet" will be

    a) "the best and the brightest" from all segments of American society.
    b) Merrill Lynch, Pierce, Fenner, and Smith.
    c) Tinkers, Evers, and Chance.
    d) Father, Son, and Holy Ghost.

19. You would be most likely to veto

    a) a large deficit budget.
    b) lowering hemlines.
    c) trading Steve Garvey.
    d) a Congressional pay raise.

20. You do NOT want to vacation in

    a) Provincetown, Mass.
    b) Key West, Florida.
    c) Fire Island, NY.
    d) New Jersey.

Scoring:

1) a - 2; b - 8; c - 5; d - 7
2) a - 0; b - 6; c - 9; d - 3
3) a - 8; b - 6; c - 8; d - 4; e - 6
4) a - 4; b - 7; c - 2; d - 8
5) a - 8; b - 2; c - 5; d - 4
6) a - 2; b - 7; c - 3; d - 6
7) a - 6; b - 6; c - 6; d - 2
8) a - 2; b - 4; c - 6; d - 6
9) a - 3; b - 1; c - 3; d - 3
10) a - 9; b - 0; c - 6; d - 6
11) a - 6; b - 6; c - 4; d - 2
12) a - 4; b - 7; c - 2; d - 2
13) a - 9; b - 0; c - 0; d - 2
14) a - 1; b - 3; c - 3; d - 2
15) a - 6; b - 1; c - 1; d - 3
16) a - 8; b - 1; c - 3; d - 4
17) a - 7; b - 6; c - 5; d - 8
18) a - 7; b - 3; c - 5; d - 4
19) a - 8; b - 0; c - 8; d - 4
20) a - 8; b - 3; c - 8; d - 2

What the Score Means:

If you chose more than one answer for the same question, it means that you are already a politician. Score yourself for as many answers as you chose. Looking ahead to see the answers earns you two more bonus points. If you had someone on your staff take the test, score three bonus points.

Everyone passes the test. The only qualification is that you bought the book.

On Your Mark!

The History Of The Presidential Primaries

Back in the Good Old Days, men didn't run for President. Campaigning was considered too undignified for the post. Abe Lincoln and Stephen Douglas changed that somewhat with their famous debates, but it still wasn't "running." Calvin Coolidge refused to leave his porch no matter how hard Teddy Roosevelt barnstormed, but unfortunately, Roosevelt established a precedent, and the Presidential Campaign was born.

Then Roosevelt did worse: he campaigned in the primaries. Happily, this didn't catch on until after World War II. The first candidate to go all out in the primaries was Wendell Wilkie in 1944. He spent fourteen hours a day for four months tromping around Wisconsin, looking for support. He didn't get a single delegate.

You would think politicians would have learned from Wendell's failure, but they applied the usual political logic: if it doesn't work at first, try it on a larger scale. So they campaigned in the primaries even harder, and Estes Kefauver, in 1952, won nine of the fourteen primaries he entered. In the Republican party, Robert Taft won the majority of the head-to-head primary confrontations with Ike. But despite Kefauver's and Taft's victories, Adlai Stevenson and Dwight D. Eisenhower were the candidates for their parties that year. Seeing as Kefauver possessed little in the way of morals, and Robert Taft had less appeal to the average voter than Barry Goldwater, you might think politicians would have second thoughts about the merits of primaries. You might, if you didn't know politicians better.

It took a Kennedy, John F., to win the primaries and make it stick. He whipped Hubert Humphrey in an early contest in West Virginia, proving that a Catholic could win in a Protestant state, and knocked Humphrey out of the race. Poor H.H.H. never knew what hit him.

Ever since then, it's been downhill, primary-wise. Jimmy Carter took it to the extreme. He was an unknown who had neither national support nor recognition, and he won both the nomination and the election. Although the Democrats have been trying to fix the system so this couldn't happen again, their "reforms" have just made the system worse. They can't figure out how to attract more voters, yet fewer candidates.

History does teach us one thing. Primaries, especially those scheduled early, tend to favor the dark-horse. This year is especially loaded. And that should be good news to you, because with this book and a little luck, you should be able to out-Carter Carter. Er, let's re-phrase that. You'll be able to make an impressive showing in any primary you choose to enter, and at least be a strong contender for Vice President. Not bad for $4.95, eh?

Becoming A Candidate: How To Get Started In Five Easy Lessons

1) **Lose Your Job**. When was the last time a man with a real job won the Presidency? Ex-governor Reagan, ex-governor Carter ... Which brings us to our next item,

2) **How To Become An Ex-Governor**, which, conveniently enough, is the title of our next book, coming soon. But don't make the mistake of becoming a Senator or an ex-Senator, unless you just like running but not winning. Have you noticed how many of them always run, yet none has won since 1960? Anyway, he was a Kennedy, not a senator.

3) **Go Away**. Always standard; even Jesse Jackson went to Europe. For some reason, if there isn't a picture of you hob-nobbing with a Queen, no matter how minor, you can't be President, or even a serious candidate.

4) **Love Thy Mother**. Another inexplicable one. So many of the candidates and Presidents have had dominant mothers: Reagan, Carter, Nixon, Abe Lincoln.

5) **Become A Nut**. It's a myth that middle-of-the-roaders always win. If you just say the same thing everyone else is saying, everybody ignores you. But if you come out in favor of giving El Salvador nuclear weapons or something bizarre, you'll attract loads of renegade millionaires who want to give you money, and dedicated fanatics who will lick your envelopes. Then, when you've taken these fanatics for their cash, take a "fact-finding trip" to El Salvador and "reassess your position."

The Job Description

From The Constitution:

Section 1. The executive Power shall be vested in a President of the United States of America. He shall hold his office during the Term of four Years... No person except a natural born Citizen, or a Citizen of the United States, at the time of the Adoption of this Constitution, shall be eligible to the Office of President; neither shall any person be eligible to that Office who shall not have attained to the Age of thirty five years, and been fourteen years a resident within the United States...

Section 2. The President shall be Commander in Chief of the Army and Navy of the United States, and of the Militia of the several States, when called into the actual service of the United States; he may require the Opinion, in writing, of the principal Officer in each of the executive Departments, upon any Subject relating to the Duties of their respective Offices, and he shall have Power to grant Reprieves and Pardons for Offenses against the United States, except in Cases of Impeachment. He shall have Power, by and with the Advice and Consent of the Senate, to make Treaties, provided two-thirds of the Senators present concur; and he shall nominate, and by and with the Advice and Consent of the Senate, shall appoint Ambassadors, other public Ministers and Consuls, Judges of the Supreme Court, and all other Officers of the United States, whose Appointments are not herein otherwise provided for, and which shall be established by Law: but the Congress may by Law vest the Appointment of such inferior Officers, as they think proper, in the President alone, in the Courts of Law, or in the Heads of Departments. The President shall have Power to fill up all Vacancies that may happen during the Recess of the Senate, by granting Commissions which shall expire at the End of their next Session.

Section 3. He shall from time to time give to the Congress Information on the State of the Union, and recommend to their Consideration such Measures as he shall judge necessary and expedient; he may, on extraordinary Occasions, convene both Houses, or either of them, and in Case of Disagreement between them, with Respect to the Time of Adjournment, he may adjourn them to such Time as he shall think proper; he shall receive Ambassadors and other public Ministers; he shall take Care that the Laws be faithfully executed, and shall Commission all the Officers of the United States.

From The U. S. Code, 1976 Edition: Title 3, Chapter 2:

102. Compensation of the President. The President shall receive in full for his services during the term for which he shall have been elected compensation in the aggregate amount of $200,000 a year, to be paid monthly, and in addition an expense allowance of $50,000 to assist in defraying expenses relating to or resulting from the discharge of his official duties, for which expense allowance no accounting, other than for income tax purposes, shall be made by him. He shall be entitled also to the use of the furniture and other effects belonging to the United States and kept in the Executive Mansion.

103. Traveling Expenses. There may be expended for or on account of the traveling expenses of the President of the United States such sum as Congress may from time to time appropriate, not exceeding $40,000 per annum, such sum when appropriated to be expended in the discretion of the President and accounted for on his certificate solely.

Real Info From The Federal Election Commission

To become a candidate for a Federal office, you must register with the Federal Election Commission. They will send you some forms and a brochure called "Candidate Registration." To save you a stamp and the taxpayers some bucks, we've reproduced the highlights of that pamphlet, word-for-word, below:

Candidate Registration
Federal Election Commission
August 1982

This brochure explains when an individual running for Federal office becomes a candidate under the Federal Election Campaign Act (the Act). It describes the steps a candidate must take to register under the Act and the steps his or her committees must take to register as political committees under the Act. Citations refer to Federal Election Commission regulations and to the Act.* Advisory opinions (AOs) issued by the Commission are cited as well. If you have any questions after reading this brochure, please call the Commission in Washington, D.C. at 523-4068 or, toll free, 800/424-9530.**

Individual Tests the Waters
Payments made to determine whether an individual should become a candidate (such as expenses for polling) do not alone

---

Commission regulations are contained in title 11 of the Code of Federal Regulations (11 CFR); the Act is contained in title 2 of the United States Code (2 U.S.C.).

**The reader should not rely solely on this brochure but should also consult the Federal Election Campaign Act and Commission regulations.*

trigger candidate status under the Act, with its registration and reporting obligations. (The $5,000 threshold that triggers candidate status is explained below.) Financial records of such activities should nevertheless be maintained because, if the beneficiary of such precandidacy activity later becomes a candidate, the funds received and payments made for "testing the waters" are considered contributions (subject to the Act's limits and prohibitions) and expenditures, and must be reported with the first report filed by the campaign. 11 CFR 100.8(b)(1).

For example, Mr. Jones is interested in running for Congress but is unsure whether he has enough support within his district to make a successful bid. He therefore accepts up to $1,000 from each of several friends to pay for an opinion poll. The results of the poll indicate good name recognition in the community, and Jones decides to run. On the first report Jones files after he becomes a candidate (i.e., after he either receives contributions or makes expenditures which exceed $5,000), his committee must report the donations from his friends as "contributions" and the costs of the poll as an "expenditure." Had Jones not become a candidate, there would have been no obligation to report these financial transactions, and the donations made to help pay for the poll would not have counted as contributions.

An individual may finance a variety of activities to test the feasibility of a potential candidacy for Federal office as long as the activities do not entail public political advertising (e.g., T.V. or newspaper ads) or represent the establishment of a campaign organization. If an individual moves beyond deciding whether or not to become a candidate and begins to plan activities to heighten his or her political appeal, he/she would become a candidate. Activities conducted over a protracted period of time might suggest, for example, campaign activity rather than testing-the-waters activity. See AOs 1981-32, 1982-3 and 1982-19.

Individual Becomes a Candidate

An individual becomes a candidate for Federal office (and thus triggers registration and reporting obligations under the Act) when his or her campaign exceeds $5,000 in either contributions or expenditures. The threshold is reached when any one of the circumstances described below occurs.

Receives Contributions or Makes Expenditures

The individual receives contributions or makes expenditures, either of which aggregate over $5,000. 11 CFR 100.3(a)(1).

Authorizes Campaign Activity

The individual authorizes another person to accept contributions or make expenditures on his/her behalf, and the authorized person receives contributions or makes expenditures which exceed $5,000. 11 CFR 100.3(a)(2).

Fails to Disavow Campaign Activity

The individual fails to write the Commission a letter disavowing unauthorized campaign efforts on his/her behalf within 30 days after being notified by the FEC that another person has received contributions or made expenditures of more than $5,000 on the individual's behalf. 11 CFR 100.3(a)(3).

Reaches Aggregate Threshold

The individual and other persons (described above), in any combination, together receive contributions or make expenditures in excess of $5,000 on the individual's behalf. 11 CFR 100.3(a)(4).

Registration by Candidate

Within 15 days after an individual becomes a candidate, he/she must designate a principal campaign committee to receive contributions and make expenditures on the candidate's behalf. This designation must be made in writing by Filing a Statement of Candidacy (FEC Form 2) or by filing a letter with the same information (i.e., the individual's name and address, the District and/or State in which Federal office is sought, the name and address of his/her principal campaign committee and the committee's campaign depository). 11 CFR 101.1(a).

Registration by Principal Campaign Committee

Within 10 days after it has been designated by the candidate, the principal campaign committee must file a Statement of Organization (FEC Form 1) with either the Secretary of the Senate or the Clerk of the House, as appropriate. The Statement must identify the committee's treasurer, bank depositories, any other committees authorized by the same candidate*** and other pertinent information, described below. 11 CFR 102.1(a) and 102.2(a).

Name of Committee

The name of the principal campaign committee must include the name of the candidate it is supporting. 11 CFR 102.14(a).

****In addition to the principal campaign committee, a candidate may designate other authorized committees to receive contributions and make expenditures on the candidate's behalf. These committees file all statements and reports through the principal campaign committee. For more information, consult the instructions on the back of the Statement of Candidacy.*

Filing The Forms

Before your can do anything in the government, you have to file a form. If you want to buy pencils, you have to file a form. If you want a raise, get the form in, first. And if you want to be President — the man who's ultimately responsible for all those forms — you have to fill out a bunch of forms.

But when you're just getting your campaign started, there are only two forms you need to file, believe it or not. For your convenience, we've enclosed the actual Federal Election Commission forms here.

STATEMENT OF ORGANIZATION

(see reverse side for instructions)

1. (a) Name of Committee (in Full) ☐ Check if name or address is changed.	2. Date
(b) Address (Number and Street)	3. FEC Identification Number
(c) City, State and ZIP Code	4. Is this an amended Statement? ☐ YES ☐ NO

5. TYPE OF COMMITTEE (check one):

☐ (a) This committee is a principal campaign committee. (Complete the candidate information below.)

☐ (b) This committee is an authorized committee, and is NOT a principal campaign committee. (Complete the candidate information below.)

Name of Candidate	Candidate Party Affiliation	Office Sought	State/District

☐ (c) This committee supports/opposes only one candidate _______________ and is NOT an authorized committee.
(name of candidate)

☐ (d) This committee is a _______________ committee of the _______________ Party.
(National, State or subordinate)   (Democratic, Republican, etc.)

☐ (e) This committee is a separate segregated fund.

☐ (f) This committee supports/opposes more than one Federal candidate and is NOT a separate segregated fund nor a party committee.

6. Name of Any Connected Organization or Affiliated Committee	Mailing Address and ZIP Code	Relationship

If the registering political committee has identified a "connected organization" above, please indicate type of organization:

☐ Corporation   ☐ Corporation w/o Capital Stock   ☐ Labor Organization   ☐ Membership Organization   ☐ Trade Association   ☐ Cooperative

7. **Custodian of Records:** Identify by name, address (phone number — optional) and position, the person in possession of committee books and records.

Full Name	Mailing Address and ZIP Code	Title or Position

8. **Treasurer:** List the name and address (phone number — optional) of the treasurer of the committee; and the name and address of any designated agent (e.g., assistant treasurer).

Full Name	Mailing Address and ZIP Code	Title or Position

9. **Banks or Other Depositories:** List all banks or other depositories in which the committee deposits funds, holds accounts, rents safety deposit boxes or maintains funds.

Name of Bank, Depository, etc.	Mailing Address and ZIP Code

I certify that I have examined this Statement and to the best of my knowledge and belief it is true, correct and complete.

Type or Print Name of Treasurer	**SIGNATURE OF TREASURER**	Date

NOTE: Submission of false, erroneous, or incomplete information may subject the person signing this Statement to the penalties of 2 U.S.C. §437g.

For further information contact: Federal Election Commission, Toll Free 800-424-9530, Local 202-523-4068

FEC FORM 1 (3/80)

STATEMENT OF CANDIDACY

(see reverse side for instructions)

1. (a) Name of Candidate (in Full)	2. Identification No.
(b) Address (Number and Street)	3. Party Affiliation
	4. Office Sought
(c) City, State and ZIP Code	5. District & State of Candidate

DESIGNATION OF PRINCIPAL CAMPAIGN COMMITTEE

6. I hereby designate the following named political committee as my Principal Campaign Committee for the ________________ election(s).
(Year of Election)

NOTE: This designation must be filed with the appropriate office listed below.

(a) Name of Committee (in Full)

(b) Address (Number and Street)

(c) City, State and ZIP Code

DESIGNATION OF OTHER AUTHORIZED COMMITTEES

7. I hereby authorize the following named committee, which is NOT my principal campaign committee, to receive and expend funds on behalf of my candidacy.

NOTE: This designation should be filed with the principal campaign committee.

(a) Name of Committee (in Full)

(b) Address (Number and Street)

(c) City, State and ZIP Code

I certify that I have examined this Statement and to the best of my knowledge and belief it is true, correct and complete.

________________________   ________________________
(Signature of Candidate)   (Date)

NOTE: Submission of false, erroneous, or incomplete information may subject the person signing this Statement to the penalties of 2 U.S.C. §437g.

CANDIDATES FOR —

President mail to:	U.S. Senate mail to:	U.S. House of Representatives mail to:		
Federal Election Commission 1325 K Street, N.W. Washington, D.C. 20463	Secretary of the Senate 119 D Street, N.E. Washington, D.C. 20510	Clerk of the House 1036 Longworth Office Bldg. Washington, D.C. 20515	**For further information contact:**	Federal Election Commission Toll Free 800-424-9530 Local 202-523-4068

FEC FORM 2 (3/80)

Getting a Date

What's the point of getting invited to the party if you don't know when it is? Here are the dates for the primaries and caucuses.

Date	State	Type	Number of Delegates
February 20	Iowa	Caucus	77
February 28	N.H.	Primary	29
March 13	Mass.	Primary	155
	Florida	Primary	191
	Alabama	Primary	83
	Georgia	Primary	112
	Oklahoma	Caucus	71
	Washington	Caucus	93
	Rhode Island	Primary	36
	Dems. abroad	Mail-in	10
	Hawaii	Caucus	36
	Nevada	Caucus	27
March 14	Delaware	Caucus	24
	Alaska	Caucus	83
March 17	Mississippi	Caucus	57
	Latin America	Caucus	10
	S. Carolina	Caucus	64
	Arkansas	Caucus	19
	Michigan	Caucus	207
	Kentucky	Caucus	84
	North Dakota	Caucus	24
March 18	Puerto Rico	Primary	71
March 20	Illinois	Primary	259
	Minnesota	Caucus	115
March 24	Kansas	Caucus	59

March 25	Montana	Caucus	33
March 27	Connecticut	Primary	80
April 7	Wisconsin	Caucus	119
	Louisiana	Primary	91
April 14	Arizona	Caucus	52
April 16	Utah	Caucus	36
April 17	Missouri	Caucus	57
April 24	Vermont	Caucus	23
	Pennsylvania	Primary	260
May 1	D.C.	Primary	25
	Tennessee	Primary	101
May 5	Texas	Caucus	267
May 7	Colorado	Caucus	68
May 8	Indiana	Primary	117
	N. Carolina	Primary	117
	Maryland	Primary	99
	Ohio	Primary	233
May 15	Nebraska	Primary	40
	Oregon	Primary	67
May 22	New York	Primary	380
May 24	Idaho	Caucus	29
	Virginia	Caucus	104
June 5	California	Primary	460
	New Jersey	Primary	163
	New Mexico	Primary	37
	South Dakota	Primary	25
	West Virginia	Primary	59

Other States:

Maine, March 4, in non-compliance, 36 delegates
Wyoming, March (date uncertain), caucus, 20 delegates
Virgin Islands, caucus, March 31, 10 delegates
Guam, caucus, April 28, 10 delegates
American Samoa, caucus, March 13, 6 delegates

Basic Tips
For Any Candidate

One of the essential traits of the successful candidate is his ability to learn from the mistakes of his predecessors. Not that he doesn't repeat those mistakes, of course, but at least he feels nostalgic while he's repeating them.

Of course, if we tried to provide you with a lesson from **all** the mistakes of past candidates, you'd be receiving a new volume of this book each month for the next 18 years. But below are some of the most glaring gaffes of the recent past, and some helpful hints for avoiding them:

How To Drive Across Bridges: Bridges have three essential elements: a left side, a middle stripe, and a right side. Try to position your car between the middle stripe and the right side. Going too far to the right can result in your ending up in the water. Going too far to the left can result in a head-on collision. Driving across a bridge should be attempted only when your mind is clear and when you have both hands on the wheel. If you experience difficulties with this procedure, call the police. Immediately.

How To Pick a Vice-President: Have your proposed running-mate look at the ink-blot below. Ask him what he sees. If he starts raving about wanting to sleep with his mother, or about being terrified of sheep, find a new running mate. Immediately.

How To Lose a Southern Accent: Listening to a dark horse with a southern drawl makes most people experience an uncomfortable sense of *deja vu*. The following schools specialize in teaching people to speak without an accent:

Charismedia Services
610 West End Ave.
New York, N.Y.

Dixon Speech Systems
138 East 36th Street
New York, N.Y.

Avoid Land Wars in Southeast Asia: If your best friend is currently losing a major land war in southeast Asia, perhaps you should consider a different career. We'll be coming out with *You Too Can Be Chairman of IBM* in a few months.

Keep Your Kids Quiet: Kids say the darndest things. But in a Presidential election, no one really cares if your children think toxic waste is "yukky" or nuclear annihilation is "gross." While they may be bright, your offspring do not make the most prestigious advisors, especially if you refer to their advice in a debate on National TV. Promise to give them a White House servant of their own if they keep their mouths shut.

Brothers Who Drink Beer and Play Softball: Should be kept on the farm.

Sheiks With Lots of Money and Funny Wires Coming Out of Their Clothes: Avoid these folks at all costs. Many of them have funny accents — the Bronx, Boston, Atlanta — and this can help you spot them immediately.

Fly Syrian Airways

"We treat you like a hero!"

New York - Damascus

    British Airways Flt. #174:
Leave NY 8:00 p.m.,
arrive London 7:40 a.m.

    Syrian Airways Flt. #404:
Leave London Tuesday or Sunday 9:45
a.m., arrive sunny Damascus 5:50 p.m.

Damascus - New York

    Syrian Airways Flt. #403:
Leave Damascus Monday at 3:30 p.m.,
arrive London at 11:25 p.m.

    Or take Flt. #401:
leave Sunday at 2:00 p.m.,
arrive London 9:55 p.m.

    British Airways Flt. #155:
leave London 11:00 a.m.,
arrive New York at 1:45 p.m.

Stay for a minimum of 7 days and enjoy our $858 round-trip fare. Fare for less than 7 days is $1548.

Get Set!

Announcing The Announcement Of The Announcement

You've decided that you want to run for President. You've filed the forms, and you've even started fund raising. But unless you tell the public of your ambitions, only your relatives will vote for you. Of course, there's an art to all this. Putting an ad in the paper that says "Vote for Me for President" just doesn't cut it anymore.

You must make The Announcement.

Don't just go off to any Ramada convention room and say "OK, that's it, I want to be Numero Uno. Vote for me for President."

Who's going to hear you? No one.

So if you're really serious about this, you've got to announce that you're going to announce that you're a candidate.

And you do that with a Press Release. We've enclosed a sample on the next page.

But wait. Announcement technology has been updated. No longer can you just announce that you're going to announce your candidacy. No, these days you must announce the Announcement of The Announcement. With this announcement, you will fuel speculation and get additional press coverage. The media will report that "Joe Candidate has announced that he will hold a press conference to discuss his political future." After this press conference, the newspapers will say, "Joe Candidate announced yesterday that he will announce the formal announcement date of his candidacy for President in the next month." Then, when you actually do kick off your campaign, return to your alma mater, declare your candidacy, and get your picture on the front page of the New York *Times*.

Every year, candidates are developing new capabilities

in announcement strategy. Candidates are beginning to leak the Announcement of The Announcement. (Since this terminology is getting a tad confusing, let's create some shorthand. The announcement of the Announcement of The Announcement will henceforth be known as "TA-TA-TA". The Announcement of The Announcement will be called "T-A^2". And the real announcement of your candidacy is just "T&A.")

At this point, we believe that a written TA-TA-TA is a bit excessive and in bad taste. This may change: a few years ago, a candidate was only allowed one announcement. But for now, if you decide to deploy your TA-TA-TA, just have someone on your staff call the local newspaper and television and radio stations, and leak the news over the phone.

If you aren't satisfied with the results of your T-A^2, or TA-TA-TA, then just cancel the press conference. This will create rumors either that you may not run, or that you're waiting for Ted Kennedy to endorse you. Then re-announce, and get some more publicity.

We told you it was an art.

Press Release

Contact: Sam Free, 203-436-4771
Release Date: PM Newspapers -- 2/1/84

NEW HAMPSHIRE--John Q. Candidate will be holding a press conference to make a major announcement concerning his political aspirations. The conference will be held on Feb. 2 at 2:00 p.m. at the Ramada Inn at First and Main St.

All members of the local media are invited to attend, but please be warned that the national press will have first priority on all space.*

Liquor and refreshments will be served.**

John (Joe) Q. Candidate
For President

---

*Of course it's a bluff, but if you were a reporter for the Wonalancet, New Hampshire *Gazette*, wouldn't you like to meet Dan Rather?

**Essential. Gin, scotch and white wine preferable.

A Free Speech

We have written your first speech for you, but we leave the choice of the actual political positions to you. The choices in the speech represent the full spectrum of Democratic ideology. Just choose the words or phrases that fit your and your audience's political philosophy.

Good evening, Ladies and Gentlemen. I am honored to be able to address you tonight. Thank you for the excellent dinner of (*fried, baked, barbecued*) chicken.

Today, we confront some of the most difficult decisions that this nation has ever faced, yet I am firmly convinced that we also have some of the greatest opportunities. We must work together to ensure that America continues to grow and prosper, together as a nation.

But first we must discuss unemployment and the other (*plagues, tragedies, calamities*) that are sweeping the nation. I (*am inexorably opposed to, abhor, am shocked by*) the level of unemployment that the current Administration continues to tolerate. I (*firmly believe, am convinced, know*) that jobs are one of this nation's highest priorities. Retraining America's workers for tomorrow's jobs is an (*essential, pivotal, crucial*) task for this country. We cannot be strong without a strong economy.

The current administration has confused a strong defense with a strong America. We cannot allow this (*grievous, major, heinous*) error to continue without correction. We are only as strong as the people themselves are. The (*unprecedented, ridiculous, shocking*) defense expenditures demanded by the Reagan Administration will only serve to (*weaken, debilitate, harm*) America. Our nation needs a (*powerful, adequate, sufficient*) defense capability, but we need not accede to every Pentagon request for a new toy.

In foreign affairs, we must continue to be (*a leader, an example, a model*) for the rest of the world, especially other democratic nations. We must support our friends and oppose our enemies. We must work for peace, not merely prepare for war. "Our nation has a sacred obligation to work for peace," as (*Franklin Roosevelt, Woodrow Wilson, John F. Kennedy*) said. But currently, we are spending (*10, 12, 14*) percent of the national budget on weapons that could destroy the planet.

Inescapably, we must deal with the issue I just referred to, nuclear (*war, holocaust, conflict*), a threat that menaces the entire earth. As the Catholic bishops (*justly, correctly, accurately*) wrote, we are morally responsible for the weapons' destructive capacity. As Bishop Berkely said, "Every man must (*face, confront, judge*) the issue of war himself; there is a sacred obligation to his fellow man." The issue is simple, ladies and gentlemen, we must work for peace with the Soviet Union, no matter how (*odious, repugnant, hateful*) their system of government may be to us.

You will hear the other major candidates during this election, (*Mr. Glenn, Mr. Cranston, Mr. Askew, Mr. McGovern, Mr. Jackson, Mr. Hollings, Mr. Hart, and Mr. Mondale*), but I hope you will remember my words. I think my (*skills, abilities, talents*), my (*experience, background, history*), and my (*belief, faith, pride*) in my fellow Americans make me unique among the candidates. I thank you for your time and your attention. Good evening.

Dress
For Electoral Success

Men: Always go with a jacket and tie, even if you're inspecting a slaughterhouse or a toxic waste site. Somehow you look more macho with your hardhat on and a butcher's blouse over your Pierre Cardin suit. It also makes it clear that you don't really work there.

Real creativity comes in deciding *how* to wear your jacket and tie. Collar unbuttoned, tie slightly loosened? Always impeccable? Jacket hung over the arm? These are going to be some of the most crucial decisions for creating an image. Let's go over the ramifications of these various approaches.

Collar unbuttoned, tie down: The hard-working, people's candidate. You're lowering your guard to the American population. You're not afraid to sweat. This look is obviously geared for the liberal.

Always impeccable: You're trying for the image of being always calm, ever unruffable. You can keep your composure even at the National Cheerleaders Convention. No matter what the situation, you're in control. Also known as "The Statesman Look."

Jacket over the arm: For the fence-sitter. A controlled people's candidate. One technical difficulty: your tie can end up in the soup or the cookie dough machine.

Cardigan sweater: Never. Brings back Jimmy Carter.

Obviously, a candidate can use all these approaches, depending on the crowd. If you're touring a factory with the executives, go for the impeccable look — show that you understand that the workers must be ruled. But the next day, touring the plant, loosen that collar, lower that tie, and be one of the guys.

Women: For many years, women's wear in politics meant dressing like your husband/boyfriend, except for far-out liberals. In essence, this meant putting on something akin to your husband's suit each morning, and adding a red bow. Also known as the Libby Dole/Jeanne Kirkpatrick Look. But some daring women, such as Colorado's Congresswoman Pat Schroeder, are actually wearing female clothes. Monitor this situation, since there is actually more potential for creativity in your outfit than your male rival's. And don't be afraid to go for the interesting gimmick. Bella Abzug was as famous for her hats as for her politics, and Millicent Fenwick employed the truly unique pipe. Perhaps jogging shoes or a well-placed sweat band could do the trick in the 80's. But resist the urge to get too trendy or kinky — definitely no "Flashdance" sweatshirts, for instance.

Politicians with gimmicks can meet big stars! Here, Barbra Streisand admires Bella Abzug's famous hat.

Fund-Raising Made Easy — Part 1

The biggest problem most new candidates face is fund-raising. All those posters and bumper-stickers and TV ads cost big bucks, and getting the money honestly is a major headache. Just ask John DeLorean.

But we have a solution. Up to now, the post of Vice-President has been filled by men with political fortunes that bolster the stock of #1. George Bush, for example, had significant experience in the Federal government and a good regional base in both the northeast and Texas. For Reagan, a Californian unknown in Washington, Bush was the perfect choice.

Political fortunes are fine, but we think that just plain fortunes can be even better. Remember, current election laws allow a candidate to contribute as much as he wants to his own campaign.

With that handy fact in mind, here are

Two Steps To No-Hassle Fund-Raising:

1) Find a very, very rich person.

2) Make him your running-mate.

If for some reason your intended running-mate balks at becoming the next #2, see if he'd like to buy a Vice-President of his very own. The old line "he's only a heart-beat away from the Presidency" should be an effective sales tactic.

Finally, if this method does not procure adequate funds, just go for commercial endorsements. Only drink Budweiser. Casually mention that you fly only American Airlines. Wear J.C. Penney clothes. Carry your *Wall Street Journal* prominently. Flash your American Express card. The possibilities are endless, and the potential windfall is huge.

Tennis players and race-car drivers do it. Why can't you?

A Slogan In Every Pot, A Chicken In Every Campaign

Every campaign must have a slogan. The public likes it because it's shorter than your campaign speech. The press likes it because it makes a good, brief way to categorize you.

Slogans have come a long way since "A Chicken in Every Pot." These days, the slogan must be all-inclusive: "The New Foundation" or "The New Beginning." That way it can cover nearly every issue, from birth control to the B-1 bomber, and is sufficiently vague. Who can be against a "New Beginning?"

Unfortunately, a lot of the good slogans are taken. Nearly every politician grabs one, and it's embarrassing if you get caught with a used, 1956 model. Some politicians are particularly greedy, and use several during their political life. Of course, Richard Nixon falls in this category.

1. Advance Agent of Prosperity
2. The People against the Bosses
3. In Gold We Trust
4. Don't Haul Down the Flag
5. Liberty, Justice and Humanity
6. The Square Deal
7. We Stand Pat
8. Let the People Rule
9. The New Freedom
10. He Kept Us Out of War
11. America First
12. Back to Normalcy
13. Courage, Confidence and Coolidge
14. Honesty at Home, Honor Abroad
15. Who But Hoover?
16. A Chicken in Every Pot
    (a Car in Every Garage)
17. Throw the Spenders Out
18. The New Deal
19. Return the Country to the People
20. A Choice for Change (and not an echo)
21. The Great Crusade
22. Peace and Prosperity
23. Crime, Corruption, Communism and Korea

24. The New Republicanism
25. Come Home, America
26. The Great Society
27. The New Frontier
28. We Never Had It So Good
29. Peace With Honor
30. Why Not the Best

The Presidential Candidate's Workout Program

Let's get credible!

If you start promising to eliminate waste, people won't believe you if you can't eliminate your own waist. So try these special Presidential exercises, especially after all those ethnic food fairs you'll have to campaign at.

The Knee Jerk — Hoist one knee at a time up to your chest at least 50 times. This exercise is to be stopped before it hurts and done without conviction.

The Waffle — Shake your head up a little, down a little, to the right, to the left. Repeat as necessary.

The PAC — Carry around large, heavy sacks of money and drop them at the feet of people who agree with you. Then threaten to pick them up again if they change their minds.

The Press Conference — Point to the right, point to the left, point to the right, inhale deeply, exhale. Duck left, duck right, look pained. Repeat for 30 minutes.

The Bleeding Heart — 300 one-handed pushups.

The Ford — Sommersaults down the stairs. Not recommended.

The Carter — Run 15 miles and collapse just as you reach the platform where the national TV cameras are set-up. Also not recommended.

The Reagan — Take a stack of *Reader's Digests* and hoist them high over the head. Lower them back down. Can be done at any time: press conferences, meetings with the Queen, etc.

The Denial — Suck in the stomach, push out the chest, inhale, exhale, squint the eyes.

The Briefing Book — (can be done with The Denial) — Shrug shoulders 15 times, grin, snicker, and say "I dunno. Boys will be boys." Five times.

The Front-Runner — Jog in place, look over the left shoulder, look over the right shoulder.

The V.P. — (for two people) — One person follows the other person around, always keeping in perfect step and repeating exactly what the other says.

Alan Cranston practices "The Carter" daily.

Presidential Running Shoes

Prevent Waffling!

Run With Firm, Purposeful Stride!

*Walk Softly While Carrying **Any** Type of Stick!*

They'll Take You To the Finish Line!

Every candidate needs a pair of these! They're durable, comfortable, and attractive without looking too chic. Plus, they'll help you reverse your direction without causing embarrassment!

(Also available in the "Gerald Ford" model — the shoelaces cannot come untied!)

Tips for Better
Media Coverage — Part 1

Charity Begins on the Campaign Trail

We started this chapter off with a clever idea: get a list of every political reporter's favorite charity. We had planned to say, "Put your money where your reporter's heart is — his favorite charity. Influence him without bribing him!"

It was a great idea. But, silly us, we learned what candidates find out so quickly: political reporters don't have any charity. We sent out two dozen letters asking the nation's top reporters to tell us their favorite charity. We got two responses, neither serious. One *Time* magazine reporter suggested that a subscription to his magazine would make a perfect gift, and the other (again, *Time*), suggested the "Jimmy Carter Society for the Encouragement of Prayer and Abstinence." Not funny, guys.

However, like most reporters we know, we never let a lack of material prevent us from writing, so we've compiled a list of some top journalists and their alma maters. Perhaps endowing a Chair in Journalism will do the trick.

Broder, David . . . . University of Chicago
and Dennison

Brokaw, Tom . . . . University of South Dakota

Buchwald, Art . . . . . University of Southern California

Donaldson, Sam . . . . . . University of Texas at El Paso

Jennings, Peter . . . . Carleton University
and Rider College

Rather, Dan . . . . Sam Houston State College

Sidey, Hugh . . . . Iowa State

Thomas, Helen . . . . Wayne State, East Michigan
State, and Ferris State

Weisman, Steven . . . . Yale University

Campaign Jargon

High Technology: Has superceded "clean industry" as America's goal. A very safe term, seeing as no one really knows what it means, and few have explored its alternatives: "low technology" or "high stupidity." Actually, it won't really employ anybody (it's all automated), and may generate more hazardous wastes, but what the heck, we need issues for 1988 (cf. "What's good for General Motors is good for America").

Unemployment: Everyone is inexorably opposed to it, especially politicians who fear they may contribute to the grim statistics if they are not perceived as being sufficiently opposed to it. But then think: an unemployed politician really isn't a politician. But on the other hand, if they win, are they really employed? Would you hire one?

Gallup and Roper: The Nielsen Ratings of politics. If you don't get good numbers, they yank you off the air.

Cutting Social Programs to the Bone: A new form of surgery invented by Ronald Reagan. Wounds cause hemorrhaging in bleeding heart liberals.

Big Government: Everyone's against it. You should be too, especially if you get on its payroll. Perhaps you could return $200 of your $200,000 paycheck.

FEC: Federal Election Committee. Runs the whole circus.

Government Industrial Policy: Currently touted by eggheads at Harvard and such as "the Democrats' strategy for the 80's." (Never mind that they're about four years late in getting a strategy.) Basically, you can think of it this way: the folks who brought you double-digit inflation, double-digit interest rates, and double-digit unemployment want to take control over the economy and run it by committee.

Nuclear Freeze: We and the Soviets will both stop building nuclear bombs. Everyone's for it, but then they throw in enough crippling reservations to make it meaningless.

Infrastructure: Usually used in the phrase "America's crumbling infrastructure." Term refers to roads and bridges, but sounds much more important.

Vegetable: Not ketchup.

Justice: Making sure your supporters get theirs. See also "equity."

Off the Record: Comments that journalists should not repeat in their reporting. As in "off the record, Charlie, I hear Candidate Smith likes to sleep with little boys."

Background: Comments that journalists can use, but will not attribute to you. When you say, "for background, I think Candidate Jones couldn't become the street-sweeper for Sioux City," it becomes "Knowledgeable sources say that Candidate Jones is not the most efficient campaigner" in the New York *Times*.

The ideal family photo for the Democratic Candidate for President. (Paste in your face and the face of your spouse.)

How To Sound
Intelligent In Iowa

There are two things to talk about in Iowa, hogs or corn. Hogs usually are the more exciting topic of the two, so we've prepared some background material so you can conduct some brilliant repartee with the Iowa voters:*

Hogs are swine, an even-toed, hoofed mammal, closely related to the peccary and the hippomatus, a member of the Artiodactyla order. (This may be a bit stuffy for your average farmer.) Hogs are omnivorous, eating insects as well as plants. Baby hogs are called *shoats*, young females are *gilts*, males are *boars*, and castrated males are *barrows*.

Hogs are great animals to raise because they grow so fast: they're ready to breed six months after they are born. Hogs have two litters a year, with a 16-week gestation period. One of the great sayings in the hog industry is that when a pig is slaughtered, "only the squeal is lost." Hog farmers use nearly every bit of the animal: the hide for leather, the stomach for tripe, the bristles for brushes, the intestines for casing processed meats, etc.

Some of the popular breeds of hogs are the Poland China (actually developed in southwest Ohio), the Duroc, the Minnesota #1, and the Bershire. The Poland China has drooping ears and six white points on the body. The Duroc is red, also with drooping ears. The Minnesota #1 was scientifically produced by geneticists at the University of Minnesota, and has erect ears and a red color. The Bershire is one of the oldest breeds, with erect ears and and a shortened snout.

** Iowa rates second only to California in agricultural products, producing twice as many hogs as any other state, and more corn. In fact, there are more hogs than humans in Iowa. If only they could vote!*

One final thought: don't run over in any hogs in your car. (Hog-aquiddick?) They have such a low center of gravity that your car will very possibly flip over the poor creature instead of running over it. This would be unpleasant for you and for the hog, and would provide a very negative photo opportunity.

Navigating
New Hampshire

New Hampshire has had the first Presidential primary in the nation for the last 32 years. The primary provides the main excitement for the state, which tells you a lot about New Hampshire.

Some people question why a small state with no large cities should play such a large role in determining who will be our next President, but you shouldn't. It's the perfect place for a dark horse candidate to stage an upset. Remember, going door-to-door in New Hampshire started Jimmy Carter along his way.

There are several essentials for a successful New Hampshire campaign. First, don't get lost. Keep the copy of the map on the opposite page with you at all times.

Second, buy long underwear. Below are two of the best outlets for the stuff:

EMS
Vose Farm Rd.
St.Peterborough, NH

L.L. Bean
6936 Casco St.
Freeport, Maine

You must be able to discuss maple syrup. As you campaign, you will note many covered buckets attached to trees. These are not mailboxes; they are receptacles for the sap. It takes 32 gallons of sap to make one gallon of syrup. If you taste the sap, you'll know why — it almost tastes like water. Residents cook it for days, boiling off the water, until the liquid reaches the proper consistency. The syrup then can be processed to make maple sugar and other products.

Novices always ask, "How is the sap flowing?" Actually, the quantity of sap is pretty consistent, year after year. What varies is the quality: good years produce a light, sweet syrup, while bad years produce a darker, bitter syrup. Graders rate the syrup on a scale of A to C depending on its quality. So be sure to show some expertise, and ask about the grade of this year's product.

A few more tips for New Hampshire:

Posing in front of the White Mountains, particularly the Presidential Range, is something every candidate should do.

Get a bumper sticker saying "This Car Climbed Mt. Washington."

Preppies should lodge at the Exeter Inn, in Exeter (phone 603-772-5901).

Drop by The State House at 107 North Main Street, in Concord. It's the home of the largest state legislature in America, and it has a collection of portraits of over 200 distinguished New Hampshire citizens. (A little briefing may be necessary before making this trip).

Visit The Friendly Farm, on Route 101 in Dublin, to kiss babies as they visit the farm animals. The animals there are usually friendlier than those on the Press Bus.

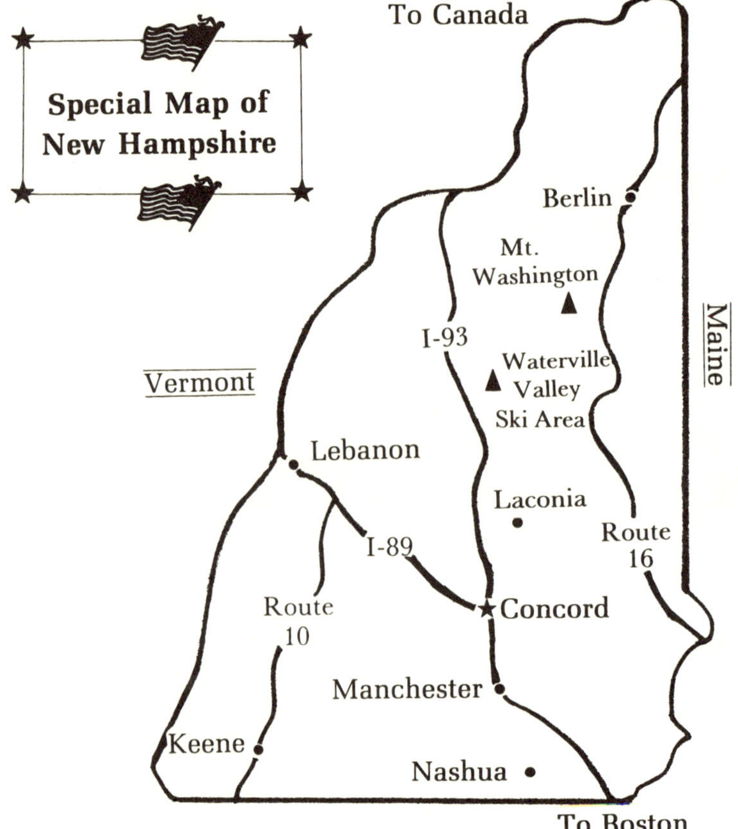

Some Take This Seriously

We've told you New Hampshire was important, but actions always speak louder than words. Here, then, is a play-by-play commentary of candidate Richard Nixon's efforts in the 1960 primaries in the tiny town of Hart's Location, New Hampshire (voting population: 12):

It was invisible, as always.

They had begun to vote in the villages of New Hampshire at midnight, as they always do, seven and a half hours before the candidate rose. His men had canvassed Hart's Location in New Hampshire days before, sending his autographed picture to each of the twelve registered voters in the village. They knew that they had five votes there, that Nixon had five votes certain — and that two were still undecided. Yet it was worth the effort, for Hart's Location results would be the first flash of news on the wires to greet millions of voters as they opened their morning papers over coffee. But from there on it was unpredictable — invisible.

From *The Making of the President, 1960,* by Theodore H. White, Pocket Books, copyright by Antheneum House.

A PAC For Everybody

Political action committees, better known as PAC's, are the latest force in politics, replacing political bosses. Like the video game, a PAC requires many quarters, but it has a nicer reward for "high score." Fortunately, you can sell out without really bothering your conscience, since groups of every political persuasion now have PAC's. Below is a list of the fifteen biggest PAC's and their contributions in the 1980 elections. Feel free to write.

Total Donated:	PAC Name and Address:
$1,536,573	Realtors PAC, 1424 N. Main St., Pueblo, CO, 81003
$1,422,731	United Auto Workers Voluntary Community Action Program, 8000 East Jefferson, Detroit, MI, 48214
$1,348,985	American Medical Pac, PO Box 28058, Washington, DC, 20005
$1,035,276	Automobile and Truck Dealers Election Action Committee, 8400 Wespark Dr., McLean, VA, 22101
$847,708	Machinists Non-partisan Political League, 1300 Connecticut Ave. NW, Washington, DC, 20006
$776,577	AFL-CIO COPE Political Contributions League, 815 16th Street NW, Washington, DC, 20006
$738,289	Committee For Thorough Agricultural Political Education of Associated Milk Producers, PO Box 32287, San Antonio, Texas, 78284

$685,248	Seafarers Political Activity Donation, 675 Fourth Avenue, Brooklyn, NY, 11232
$681,370	United Steelworkers of America Political Action Fund, Five Gateway Center, Pittsburgh, PA, 15222
$652,370	National Association of Life Underwriters PAC, 1922 F Street NW, Washington, DC, 20006
$647,875	American Dental PAC 1101 17th St., NW Suite 1006 Washington, DC 20036
$614,795	MEBA Political Action Fund 444 North Capitol St. Suite 800 Washington, DC 20001
$592,960	American Bankers Association 1120 Connecticut Ave., NW 7th Floor Washington, DC 20036
$584,144	Transportation Political Education League—CNA 146000 Detroit Ave. Cleveland, OH 44107
$565,125	Active Ballot Club 1775 K St., NW Wahington, DC 20006

Source: *The PAC Directory*

A Polished Poll

There are straw polls and exit polls and Gallups and Ropers and the New York Times/CBS and God knows what else. Well, now there's a John Q. Candidate Poll. You should find that it will come in handy, when you get results from the other polls:

1. Is the name John Q. Candidate familiar to you? (Only asked to family members.)

a) Yes .... b) No

2. Do you favor a candidate like John Q. Candidate who wants peace, prosperity, and better weather?

a) Yes .... b) No

3. Would you vote for a candidate with those views?

a) Yes .... b) No

4. Are you tired of the current ineptitude and corruption in Washington?

a) Yes .... b) No

5. Aren't the rest of the Democratic candidates a bunch of bozos?

a) Yes .... b) No

6. Would you like to apply for an American Express card? (See the chapter on fund raising.)

a) Yes .... b) No

7. Would you vote for John Q. Candidate if his life depended on it?

a) Yes .... b) No

Poll Results: 80% of those polled recognized the name of John Q. Candidate. (Your kid sister disowned you.) 78% supported his views, saying they would would vote for a candidate holding those views. The majority said they were displeased with the current administration and did not consider John's Democratic rivals strong candidates. They said that if John Q. Candidate were strongly interested in the office of the presidency, they would vote for him.

The next step: prepare a press release heralding the results of the poll, and distribute it to all the major news media. If you have the time, make a nice chart for *USA Today.*

Great Moments In Political Rhetoric

"Are you aware that Claude Pepper is known all over Washington as a shameless extrovert? Not only that, but this man is reliably reported to practice nepotism with his sister-in-law, and he has a sister who was once a thespian in wicked New York. Worst of all, it is an established fact that Mr. Pepper, before his marriage, practiced celibacy."

From the 1950 Florida Senatorial Democratic Primary, remarks by George Smathers. Smathers won the primary, and then the general election. We draw no conclusions from this.

The Committee to Elect

★★★ John Q. Candidate ★★★

President

```
Mr. Hugh Hefner
Playboy Magazine
1215 River Street
Chicago, Illinois   60603

Dear Hugh,

     Thank you for your inquiry.

     I regret that I cannot be interview-
ed by your magazine. I appreciate the
national exposure it would give me
(alongside your other types of expo-
sure), but my media advisers tell me
it would be an ill-considered move.
Both Jimmy Carter and Ed Koch con-
firmed this opinion for us.

     However, could we further discuss
using your 1983 centerfolds in my
transition team?

     Thanks again for the offer.

                    Sincerely,



                    John Q. Candidate
```

202-555-1984
1601 Pennsylvania Avenue, Washington, DC 20010
★★★

Paid for by the Commitee to Elect John Q. Candidate President

Go!

Official Campaign Identification

This is to certify that

____
PLEASE PRINT

is an official Democratic Candidate for President, and is entitled to all the rights and privileges thereof.

Signed: ___________________________________

Expires: 11/02/84.

Famous Slightly Dirty Tricks

We're not recommending these, of course, but at least they make interesting reading.

1) **Buy a Little Television Time Before Your Opponent's Major Speech.** In a New Jersey campaign, the two candidates were showing their hour-long presentations at 10:00 p.m. and 11:00 p.m. These two films were the highlights of their candidacy. The candidate at the 10:00 slot ended his film with five minutes of test pattern. All the viewers assumed that the television was over for that night, and they switched off their sets. The second candidate lost in a landslide. This trick could be updated by using a thirty second commercial, announcing that "Bowling For Towels" will be the next show.

2) **Get Mobbed By Admirers.** Thousands attended John F. Kennedy rallies in 1960, often overwhelming the security precautions. The crowds made it look like Kennedy was the "people's choice" over the unglamorous Richard Nixon. Although it has been repeatedly denied, it seems that many of those wooden barricades that were supposed to hold back the crowds had been sawed three-quarters of the way through. With the slightest pressure, the crowd would come bursting through, making for great television.

3) **The Old Foreign Language Routine.** Richard Nixon attracted an enthusiastic crowd into a narrow Chinatown street. Banners in English and Chinese welcomed him to the area. Well, the English ones did, at least. The Chinese banners asked questions about the allegedly unscrupulous loans from a defense contracter to Nixon's brother. A Democratic operator had put up the Chinese signs.

Tips For Better Media Coverage — Part II

Campaign Stunts

As we have tried to emphasize, the quickest way to become a front-runner in the primaries is to command the attention of the media. Doing this requires some creativity, true, but mostly slyness and an almost treacherous frame of mind. And since your opponents are all professional politicians — people who have pretty well cornered the market on slyness and treachery — you've got a tough job ahead of you.

Below, we've assembled some basic campaign stunts (although you should refer to them as "creative out-reach concepts" or something) that should get you plenty of exposure. Remember, these are just a few ideas; use them to spur your creativity — and your candidacy — to new heights.

1) **Exploit A Sport.** JFK played touch football and sailed, Nixon played golf, Ford hit the ski slopes (literally), Carter jogged and played softball, and Reagan rides horses. Their athletic accomplishments reassured the populace that the President was a robust, regular guy. At the very least, you need a sport because of the great photo opportunities. But have all the good ones been taken?

Emphatically, no! To our knowledge, no president has been involved in one of America's most popular spectator sports, Professional Wrestling. At auditoriums around the country and on TV sets every Saturday morning, millions of voters cheer as Andre the Giant sends the Fearless Samoans, the Doctor of Death, or some other wicked hulk into the turnbuckles. And the fans are intensely loyal — they always cheer the wrestlers considered good, and they always hiss the ones considered bad.

So, you need to create a personna for yourself, instantly recognizable as good (how about "Prince of Prosperity"?), and publicly challenge Walter Mondale, John Glenn, et al. to a three-rounds, no-holds-barred match. Or, better yet, if you have a prospective running-mate, go for the tag-team title. (This is a good way to weed-out wimp running-mates, too.)

Of course, the other Democrats will fail to show for their matches, giving you the opportunity to rant and rave into the camera on "Championship Wrestling" on Saturday morning. "This guy wants to be the Leader of the Free World, and he won't even step into the ring with me!" you snort. "I want you, Walter Mondale, and you, John Glenn, and I'll take you both at the same time!" you bellow as you shake your fist at the camera.

And don't worry about fair play and clean holds and such. Wrestling fans aren't too big on stuff like that.

2) **Utilize New Media.** Franklin D. Roosevelt, with his "fireside chats," was probably the first President to effectively utilize a new communication medium, radio. And John F. Kennedy was the first to understand the effect television exposure could have on his candidacy. Your task, then, is to find a new medium, and exploit it to your best advantage.

Thus, you need to create the first "political video" and arrange for it to be played on MTV at least once an hour. You can make a good video for $50,000 or so, and the air time is free. Since no one with cable watches regular commercials anymore — they all flip to MTV during the breaks — you can put all that TV ad money into MTV and quadruple your effectiveness. You'll be perceived as "hip" with the young voters (especially if you hire a hot back-up band, like The Clash, Talking Heads, or The Go-Go's), and the other media will refer to you as "a pioneer in public communications," "a technological wizard," etc.

By the way, if you don't know how to play an electric guitar, at least learn how to fake it.

For more information, write Warner Amex Communications, MTV Division, 1133 Sixth Ave., New York, NY, 10036.

3) **Hit The Guest Star Circuit.** Again, the key here is cheap, non-commercial exposure. Apply to every game show on TV and offer your services as a guest panelist. Game show celebrities are household names to millions of voters. You could be one of them, and you might also win some lovely patio furniture, to boot.

The second possibility here is to book passage on America's favorite cruise ship, "The Love Boat." If you're concerned about your acting abilities, you needn't worry — no one else on the show seems to care. Anyway, you could play yourself: a dedicated, good-hearted Average Citizen who wants to get into the White House and make this country great again. You're just taking a quick vacation on the *Pacific Princess* before launching your all-out political assault.

A quick warning, though: we've heard rumors that "Vicki," the Captain's daughter, has applied to be a Congressional page. Stay on the opposite end of the boat from her.

4) **Become The Human Fly.** The media loves the daring stunts of Phillipe Petit and Dan "Spiderman" Goodall. When they scale the world's tallest buildings or walk across Niagara Falls on a tightrope, the cameras follow their every move.

So, we suggest you take a few lessons from these guys, buy some climbing equipment, and start scaling. For starters, how about the Renaissance Center in Detroit, or the Hancock Building in Boston? About three-fourths of the way up, you'll need to unfurl a huge "Vote For John Q. Candidate" banner and hang it from an inaccessible place.

Of course, you'll want to save your grand finale — climbing the Washington Monument — until the key primaries.

Presidential Physics

Believe it or not, the political process is subject to the same physical laws as the rest of the universe. Well, sort of...

The First Law: A politician keeps running for office until investigated by a grand jury.

The Second Law: When two politicians of equal stature and experience collide, the one with the better media consultant wins.

The Third Law: When three different-sized politicians are dropped from a window, they all land at the same time, but only a Presidential candidate will go back and do it again and again until the television cameramen are satisfied.

The Fourth Law: Candidates rotate around NBC, ABC and CBS, not vice versa.

The Fifth Law: Kansas really is flat.

The Law of Relativity: What plays in Boise may not play in Boston.

The Law of Thermodynamics: On a cold night, a Democratic candidate for President giving a speech is better than a space-heater.

High-Tech Press Releases

The day of the press release is over. You can save yourself and the newspaper a lot of time by writing **and** typesetting the story yourself.

Below, we've done the work for the two most important papers for you. We also have filmed segments with Dan Rather, David Jennings, and Tom Brokaw announcing your candidacy, but obviously, we couldn't enclose these tapes with the text. Just send $75,000 to R.J. Publications, 4651 Yale Station, New Haven, CT, 06520, and we'll send you the tapes. And please, no unmarked bills smaller than twenties.

For The New York Times:

Dark Horse To Enter Race For Democratic Nomination

By HOWELL CLINES
Very Special to the New York Times

CONCORD, N.H. — Before a large crowd of cheering supporters, John Q. "Joe" Candidate formally announced that he was a Democratic candidate for President.

Mr. Candidate, 35, joins the field of seven other candidates in the race for the Democratic nomination.

Mr. Candidate pledged that fairness and equity will be the hallmarks of his campaign. "I don't want this nomination unless I win it fair and square," he said. "But I plan to trample Mondale, Glenn and those other suckers into the ground."

His experience as chief sanitation engineer for Wilmark, North Dakota, makes him the man to watch, he said.

"Picking up those cans every morning at 5:00 a.m. leads to some pretty heavy thoughts," he said.

Political pundits give Mr. Candidate a strong chance in the primaries, considering him the beer-drinker's candidate. Insider polls show him with high name recognition and surprising support.

Mr. Candidate said his campaign will center around a lower defense budget while maintaining a "strong defense," lower taxes, more responsive government, and better weather.

For USA Today:

USA's Candidate Hits Campaign Trail

By Marilyn Fink
USA TODAY

CONCORD, N.H. — It all started when John Q. (Joe) Candidate was watching Monday Night Football. His wife shouted, "Hey, Joe, who do you think you are, the President or something? Go empty the garbage!"

Joe thought, "Why not?"

And at his kickoff press conference in New Hampshire, Candidate made it formal in front of a wildly enthusiastic crowd.

"I'm going to trash those other suckers," Joe said. He said he plans to campaign mainly by guest appearances on *The Love Boat* and soap operas.

Around the USA, voters were reacting to Candidate's announcement with a high degree of support.

"I like the guy, yessir," Milt Bonks, a dairy farmer in Ohio, USA, commented. "Anyone that wants to do something about this weather in the USA is OK with me."

The Issues

Here's a quick run-down on the issues that you might face on the campaign trail. We feel that if you want any chance of being elected, you must take the stands we suggest. As you can see, there is no "undecided" category. Real politicians always take a stand.

	For	Against
Unemployment:		★
Bureaucracy:		★
Governmental Waste:		★
Cutting Social Programs:		★
High Technology:	★	
Strong Defense:	★	
Cutting Defense "waste":	★	
Solidarity:	★	
Socialism:		★
Racism:		★
A Black Presidential Candidate:		★
Pollution:		★
A Proud America:	★	
Alternative Energy:	★	
Education:	★	
Justice:	★	
The U.S.F.L. (unless you own a franchise):		★
The Designated Hitter:		★
Retraining Workers:	★	
Freedom:	★	
God:	★	
The Moral Majority:		★
Baseball:	★	
Motherhood:	★	
Low-Calorie Apple Pie:	★	

	For	Against
Abortion		
morally:		★
as government policy:	★	
Protectionism:		★
Foreign Cars:		★
The Elderly:	★	
The Youth:	★	
Their Parents:	★	
Any Other Age Group:	★	
The Poor:	★	
The Rich		
in public speeches:		★
as Contributors:	★	
Investment:	★	
Rebuilding "our crumbling infrastructure":	★	
Taxes:		★
"Astronomical" Deficits:		★
A Crushing Handshake:		★
George Steinbrenner:		★
Fried chicken:	★	
Ethnic foods:	★	
Alka-Seltzer:	★	

Fund-Raising Made Easy — Part 2

How To Bury the Skeletons In Your Closet and Make Big Money, Too!

Unless you and your family have lived on a remote island all your lives, you've probably accumulated some potentially embarrassing secrets, commonly called "skeletons in the closet." Every politician has a few, and they all have nightmares about some snooping reporter revealing those hard-to-bury gaffes.

But, in our never-ending quest to keep you one step ahead of the political pack, we've devised a fool-proof method of eliminating those skeletons — *and making money in the process!* It's really so simple, we're surprised someone didn't think of it before. Just follow these simple steps:

1) Write down every detail of the five most embarrassing stories in your life — drugs, sex, mental health problems, whatever. If it would look horrible on the front page of the New York *Post*, write it down. Feel free to embellish luridly, too.

2) Contact:

The Star
730 3rd Ave.
New York, NY 10017

The National Enquirer
Lantana, FL 33464

3) Sell your complete story (to be run in weekly installments) to the higher bidder.

4) Hold out for at least $75,000, give them your stories, and relax.

"Relax?!" you say. "How can I relax when my most intimate, humiliating secrets will soon be revealed to millions of voters waiting in supermarket lines?!"

No problem. First of all, do you think anyone with an IQ over 12 really **believes** anything those rags report? Of course not. And the wilder the story, the less credibility they have.

Second, when some legitimate reporter **does** uncover the facts about the week you spent in Bermuda with the soap opera sex symbol, there's no way his paper can print it, because they'd have to admit that they were scooped by *The National Enquirer*. Can you really see the New York *Times* saying, "Democratic presidential contender John Q. Candidate, as reported first in *The National Enquirer*, spent two weeks with Prince Andrew's former girlfriend..." Or how about the *Wall Street Journal* printing, "According to *The Star*, Joe Candidate financed his Princeton education by selling drugs and term papers to his classmates..." It just doesn't look right.

So, like we said, relax. Your worst secrets have been reported to the last detail, and no one cares. Plus, they can't get any more dirt on you, and you just made a tidy profit.

P.S. 10% should adequately express your appreciation to us.

"Hey Martha,
Look What I Found
In the Garage!"

We don't know what you would want to do with the item
on the opposite page.* Of course, you would *not* want
to send it to:

Mr. William Casey, Director
Central Intelligence Agency
Langley, VA

Nor would you want to send to

David Stockman, Director
Office of Management and Budget
1325 E Street
Washington, DC

Of course, if you accidentally sent it to either of these
two fellows, you certainly wouldn't want to tell:

Lou Cannon, reporter
The Washington Post
1150 15th Street
Washington, DC

or

Jack Anderson Enterprises
1401 NW 16th Street
Washington, DC

about your little accident.

We supplied the cover. We'll let you decide what should
go inside. Be creative.

Presidential Briefing Book

★★★★

CONFIDENTIAL

★★

TOP SECRET

★★

EYES ONLY

★★★★

Endorsements

Thanks to us, you only need one!

Unfortunately, by the time you got this book, most of the important groups have already endorsed one of your opponents, probably Mondale. The big labor unions, the teachers, old politicians — these guys, heavy-weights in the endorsement business, are already committed, so there's no use wasting your time on them.

Fortunately, there's one superstar that every politician has overlooked, and you should promise *anything* to snag him. Of course, we're talking about the inimitable Mr. T.

That's right. Mister Period T, the fearsome-but-tender actor who threatened most of America into watching his absurd TV show. This bodyguard-turned-star virtually saved NBC singlehandedly in the Nielsen ratings. Imagine what he could do for your campaign.

For starters, you'd steal 90% of Jesse Jackson's votes and thunder. Second, you'd impress all those guilty, liberal whites who buy Mr. T's spiel about how his jewelry and chains "symbolize the chains my people was kept in by the slave-owners." Third, Mr. T would simply bully thousands into voting for you. And, fourth, you'd get a great bodyguard fairly cheap.

Imagine this TV commercial:

(Mr. T, in all his glory, has his arm around you)

You: *Hi, I'm John Q. Candidate. I'm a Democratic candidate for President, and I'd like you to meet one of my biggest supporters.*

Mr. T: *(growling)* I pity the fool who don't vote fo' my good friend John Candidate. Candidate watches my A-Team show every week, and he saw "Rocky III" seventeen times, so he's obviously the best man fo' President,

and you know it. Reagan's a dummy, and we need to
get him outta that White House and onto my TV show
so's I can snarl at him and punch his face, and we need
to make Candidate here the President. You hearin' me,
America? So pull that lever marked 'Candidate' or I'll
pull your arms outta their sockets. Oh, yeah, and send
some money to my friend, too, fool.''

Mr. T is political dynamite! Write to him in care of NBC,
Rockefeller Center, New York.

Mr. T: political dynamite!

Candidate Assertiveness Training:

Island Invading

Democrats of the recent past often have not fared well in tests of assertiveness. John F. Kennedy flexed U.S. muscle at the Bay of Pigs, now commonly referred to as "the Bay of Pigs fiasco." Johnson's display of toughness got America into the most unpopular war in American history and sparked a decade of inflation. And Carter's lack of aggresiveness in dealing with the Iranian hostage crisis earned him the general epithet "wimp."

Republicans, on the other hand, have received high marks and garnered wide public support for their assertive efforts. The public went wild when Ford rescued the Mayaguez and cheered when Reagan "saved" the med students and democracy in Grenada.

So, you need to prove that Democrats can be macho, too. Taking a tip from Reagan's success, we suggest you try this approach:

Send about 15 members of your staff to a small, remote Caribbean island, preferably populated with 50 or so natives with a sense of humor and a need for cash. Claim the trip is a "retreat," a strategy-planning session for the key staffers. Of course, send out a press release announcing the "working vacation."

After two days, claim that "dozens" of Marxist cannibals are holding your staff hostage on a collective farm. The "cannibals," of course, are simply the natives being paid to act like terrorists for a week or so. Issue an Emergency Press Release (see Release A) stating that you and your key aides will be leaving to rescue your devoted, terrified staff.

You'll need to charter a few boats — your "Freedom Flotilla" — and get a bunch of M-80's, smoke bombs, flares, and blank pistols. Then, when the press photographers are safely on the island and all set up, make a dramatic beach landing, set off lots of fireworks and flares, rush into the building where your staff is being held, and "overpower" the guards.

After you have freed your staff, hold a press conference on the beach, and announce the great victory for freedom. Be sure that there are some black smudges on your face and that your hair is messed up. And loosen your tie. A few staffers should then hug you, weep for joy, and describe to the reporters what a terrible ordeal they went through. Offer to keep a few staff members on the island to "assist the natives in learning the fundamentals of democracy and freedom."

Then, announce the time of the helicopter air-lift (choppers make great TV), get all your people off the island, and steam back to the U.S.

Make sure you plan the assault in the morning, and finish everything by early afternoon, so the TV reporters can have plenty of time to prepare their reports for the 6:00 p.m. news.

You will most likely be met at the port by thousands of cheering Americans, and the next few days you'll be riding in ticker-tape parades in the major markets, er, cities. Be sure to emphasize that although you're "a man of peace who abhors the use of force to solve problems," you "can only be pushed so far."

Next invasion: the White House!

Press Release

Contact: Sam Free, 203-436-4771
Release Date: PM Newspapers

<u>E M E R G E N C Y</u>

WASHINGTON--The key staff assistants to John Q. Candidate, Democratic Candidate for President, are being held hostage by a desperate group of Marxist cannibals on the tiny island of Mnentubo, Candidate reported today. The staffers were on the island for a week-long strategy retreat.

The natives have vowed to sacrifice the Americans to their god Lenin, and then eat their remains, unless their demands are met. According to the natives, the staffers are now being forced to do hard labor on their collectivized farm.

Candidate announced today that he will attempt a bold rescue operation,

(MORE)

John (Joe) Q. Candidate
For President

beginning at sundown tomorrow night. He has organized a flotilla of loyal supporters who own boats, and he will attempt to storm the island at sunrise.

The press is welcome to join the flotilla, and there will be a special aide for each photographer to assist in geting dramatic angles. Refreshments will be served en route. NOTE: The assignment will be hazardous, so please take proper precautions. A basic map is below:

Mnentubo Island

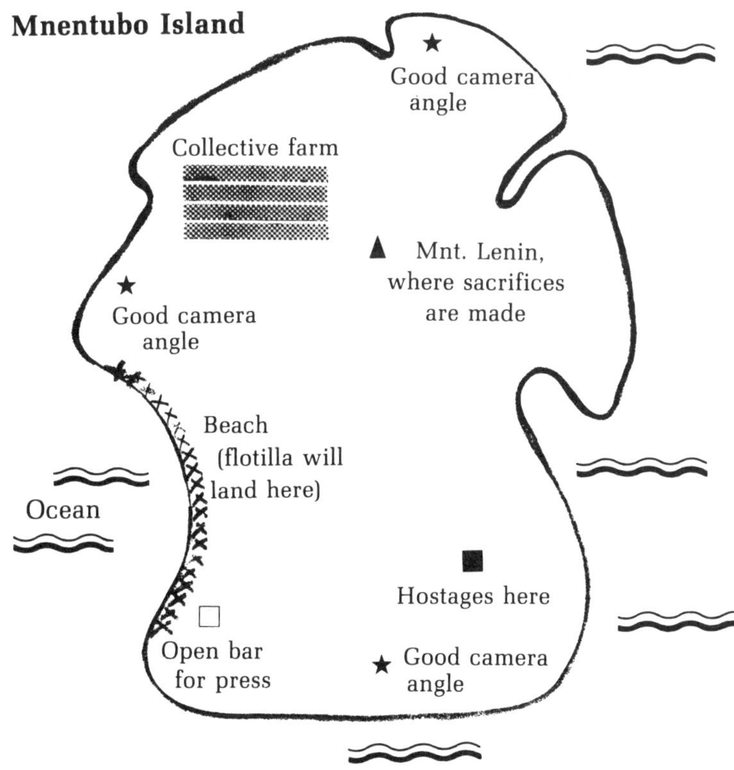

Fun For The Rest
Of The Family

Not much can relieve the monotony of the media's coverage of the candidates when the primaries get under way. Watching the nightly "Election '84" stories is quite similar to long-distance driving: you pass familiar landmarks (Iowa, New Hampshire, progressively nasty debates); you watch for the important signs (polls, financial disclosures, endorsements); and all the time you're praying for the trip to end soon.

When Dan Rather says, "It's day 51 of the primary campaign, and John Q. Candidate, victor of the last three primaries, today condemned President Reagan for...," it's really not too different from hearing, "Daddy, how much farther?" or seeing "Welcome to the New Jersey Turnpike; New York 110 miles."

To reduce the tedium of long road trips, drivers have devised highway games. The candidates and the voting public can also try to relieve the boredom of their long Presidential journey by playing some of the election games we have devised below:

Alphabet Soup

When local television stations supply footage to the national news, their call letters (WXYZ, or whatever) appear in the corner of the screen or at the end of the newscast. The object of this game is to get all the letters of the alphabet by using the call letters of local stations on the national news. For example, WABC gives you the letters W, A, B, and C. The first person to see all 26 letters wins.

The expert version of this game require players to get the letters **in order**. That is, you cannot get G until you have seen F. Thus, WABC would give you A, B and C, but you would have to get to V before you could use the W.

Catch That Phrase

The first person to hear a candidate or reporter use **all** of the following phrases wins.

1. "Momentum has shifted"
2. "Hard-fought campaign"
3. "I (he, she) would never stoop to..."
4. "My esteemed colleague"
5. "Too close to call"
6. "Issues-oriented campaign"
7. "My loyal wife/husband"
8. "The ballooning deficit"
9. "All my dedicated supporters"
10. "Dark-horse candidate"
11. "Our crumbling infrastructure"
12. "On the backs of the poor"
13. "No comment"
14. "Fiscal irresponsibility"
15. "Insensitive to the plight of..."
16. "A disappointing finish"

Catch That Scene

The first person to see a candidate on television in **all** of the following scenes wins.

1. Milking a cow.
2. Standing in front of a white church.
3. Shaking hands at a factory.
4. Walking through a high-tech factory.
5. Kissing a baby.
6. Eating a chicken dinner.
7. Exiting an airplane.
8. Smiling with his family.
9. Cutting a ribbon.
10. Showing weariness by rubbing eyes, snoozing on the plane, etc.

Presidential Baseball

Politics and baseball are both great American pastimes, so why not combine them? Pretend you're at the ballpark when you read the paper or watch the news, and score the "game" accordingly. Arbitrarily divide the candidates into two teams — for example, Glenn, Cranston, and Mondale versus Hart, Hollings, and Ted Kennedy (yes, he counts — play him like a designated hitter).

Then play the game by the usual baseball rules — three outs per side, etc. Feel free to devise your own criteria for hits, outs, etc., but to give you an idea, we've described some of our sample scoring:

Single:

- Being the first candidate mentioned on the nightly news.
- Leading the polls that day.
- Receiving a standing ovation in a crowd of 5,000 or more

Double:

- Being endorsed by the governor of the state in which he/she is campaigning.
- Getting endorsed by a local labor union with more than 2,000 members.
- Getting a famous author, singer, or movie star to work on the campaign.
- Having another candidate respond to your attacks.

Triple:

- Breaking $5.0 million in campaign contributions.
- Being called the "front-runner" by Dan Rather.
- Being on the cover of a national news magazine.

Home Run:

- Winning a primary.
- Discovering financial improprieties in an opponent's campaign.

One Strike:

- Being called the dark horse.
- Mispronouncing a local politician's name.

Two Strikes:

(These give the candidate two strikes at one time)

- Dan Rather mispronounces your name.
- Being last in the polls.
- Not getting mentioned in that evening's news.
- Agreeing to a *Playboy* interview.

Out:

- Campaign manager resigns for alleged anti-Semitic remarks.
- Spouse admits he/she smoked marijuana.
- Candidate forgets what state he/she is in.

Ejected from the game:

- Spouse has herpes.
- Getting caught accepting illegal campaign contributions.

★★★ John Q. Candidate ★★★
President

```
Mr. Bruce Jacobsen
Mr. Rollin Riggs
4651 Yale Station
New Haven, CT      06520


Dear Bruce and Rollin,

     How would you like to manage
my general election campaign?

     The standard $100,000.00,
apiece, will apply, of course.

     Many thanks, and I look
forward to hearing from you as
soon as possible.


     Sincerely,




John Q. Candidate
```

Conceding with Class

Someone once said, "Show me a good loser, and I'll show you a loser."

But he neglected the corollary to that bit of wisdom: "Show me a sore loser, and I'll show you someone that everybody despises."

It's a basic truth in politics that losers must be nice about it. They cannot act shell-shocked and say, "Gee, how could this happen to me?" They cannot be bitter and rave about corruption and media bias and all that. (The Richard Nixon syndrome).

If, through some bizarre quirk of fate, you lose your bid for the Democratic nomination,* you must bravely face the grim realities of the situation, concede gracefully, and stride off, seemingly more determined than ever to "get 'em next time."

With this in mind, we now offer some help for your "worst-case scenario." You lost. The struggle has proved pointless (though hopefully profitable). The papers will report your concession speech, maybe run an appropriately sad photo, and then you're nobody, an Average Citizen once again. It's a tough day for anyone: you despise your louse of an opponent, but you're expected to be a good sport, offer your congratulations and assistance, and then fade into the sunset. "Well, I just blew my life's savings, alienated all my friends, and disappointed my sick mother, but, hey, no problem. I'm just happy to have been able to participate in our great democratic process, and I'll be thrilled to do anything I can to help my worthy opponent make this country great again."

Right. It's tough, but you've got to do it if you ever want to be regarded as a higher life form again.

You have to concede gracefully, get your digs in very subtly, and leave room for further political maneuver-

---

No, we won't refund your money for this book if you lose.

ings (i.e., the Vice-Presidency).

The following speeches should satisfy everyone. The first speech was written to assuage your burning desire to call your opponent a worthless, corrupt slug. The second is the one you actually give. Try not to confuse them.

The Speech You Wish You Could Deliver:

Hello,

I have come here to concede the nomination to (*insert name*) and to thank my friends and staff for their work during the campaign. However, as I look out over the audience, I see a lot of people whom I've never laid eyes on before, and I assume they're trying to pass themselves off as either staff or friends, when actually they're just mooching free *hors d'oeuvres* and drinks. But it's no problem, because we just hocked all the women's furs from the coat room.

Yes, we lost. Lost bad. Maybe if I had played professional football and been a POW like (*insert name*) I would have had a chance. Except for the fact that his family's oil money has been funding candidates for 40 years and that his brother runs the ad agency that produced the Federal Express commercials, he had nothing at all going for him, and everyone knows it.

Who, me bitter? Just because I lost my job, all my friends, my house, my car, my health? Financial security and a pleasant social life are for wimps. Hell, I'm really all choked-up with gratitude to my country for allowing me to participate in our government. American democracy: where your staff tells you that instead of going out to give speeches, you should use the money for 30-second television spots.

Mostly, though, I'd like to give the credit for this loss to my incompetent staff, who wouldn't know a columnist from a communist. They thought the FEC was a new football league, and one of them was convinced that the Op-Ed Page was a kinky kid who runs errands for Congressmen. By making personal calls to old lovers all over the country, my staff managed to rack up a phone bill greater than the gross national product of Belgium. Thanks, troops: I'll send my kids to work for *your* campaigns. And you guys can certainly count on me for job recommendations. I have a good friend who runs a road-paving company in Times Beach, Missouri, and I hear he's hiring.

The Speech You Actually Give

My dedicated staff, friends, family, and reporters:

For many of us, this is perhaps the most disappointing moment of our lives. In a few hours, we watched months of strenuous, dedicated work go down the drain. Many of us have spent untold hours each day in an effort which now seems worthless.

But was it really all for nothing?

I think not. Without people like us — people who care deeply for the great democratic traditions of this country — our political process would deteriorate. Through our campaign, we have broadened the horizons of the American voter, introduced new, necessary ideas into the political mainstream, and demonstrated that, even in the realm of wealthy lobbies, corruption, and slick, Madison Avenue politicians, the little guy, the Average Citizen with a deep love for his country, can indeed make a difference.

Yes, there are problems in this process, even within our own party. We all know what they are, and we all know who benefits from them. But we have demonstrated our strength by mounting an effective campaign, and we now can use this strength to advance reforms in the system.

So, what's next? Well, I pledge my full assistance and co-operation to our party's nominee, (*insert name*). The Democratic Party has a difficult election ahead, and I fully believe that (*insert name*) needs all the help he can get, and he can certainly count on me.

And you, my friends, you who have served me so well,

often uncompensated — except for the occasional personal long-distance phone call from headquarters (pause for embarrassed laughter) — I can assure you that I will not forget your dedicated, unselfish efforts, and I promise that I will do everything I can to help you secure the positions or jobs you want when you leave this campaign. In fact, go ahead and write your own recommendations — just leave a blank for me to sign my name!

Before we go our separate ways, I hope that each of you understands one thing: we are all winners. We are winners simply because we played the game. We didn't just sit back and passively watch the passing parade, watch our lives be affected by people doing things to us. We participated, and we can always be proud of that.

Well, even though I'm no longer a politician, I still feel the urge to make long speeches. (laughter) However, I don't know much more to say. I'm tired, and I know you're tired, so perhaps we should just say *au revoir* and see what tomorrow brings.

Good night, and God bless.

Is George McGovern joking, or what?

The person who sends us the best answer will receive a copy of Jimmy Carter's classic campaign book, Why Not the Best? Mail your answer to RJ Publications, 4651 Yale Station, New Haven, CT, 06520.

Deadline: June 5 (the final primaries).

Presidential
Baseball
Cards

Collect them all !!
Trade them with your friends !!

GARY HART
Batted .375 managing
McGovern in '72

JOHN GLENN
Right Stuff;Wrong Staff

REUBIN ASKEW
Reubin who?

JESSE JACKSON
Politics' Jackie Robinson

Though not particularly experienced, could be a solid player

Stats: Born July 18, 1921

Minor Leagues: Muskingum
College

Electoral Percentages: 1980   69%
                                  1974   65%
(all in the Senate League)

Quote: ''I don't look at myself as
being oriented in any one particular direction.''

Gary's trying to move from a
managing position to active duty

Stats: Born November 28, 1937

Minor Leagues: Bethany College,
Yale

Electoral Percentages: 1980   50%
                                  1974   57%
(all in the Senate League)

Quote: Says his generation is
not ''a bunch of little Hubert
Humphreys.'' .

May become the Jackie Robinson
of Presidential politics

Stats: Born October 8, 1941

Minor Leagues: Baptist College

Electoral Percentages: Rookie

Quote: ''A black man should be
President.''

Many expected him to be a starter
in 1976, but rookie Jimmy Carter
took his spot

Stats: Born September 11, 1928

Minor Leagues: Florida State,
University of Florida

Electoral Percentages: 1974   61.2%
                                  1970   56.8%
(both in the Gubernatorial League)

Quote: ''The country needs a
southern Governor.''

ALAN CRANSTON
Veteran Player

ERNEST HOLLINGS
Jimmy Carter's Speak-Alike

WALTER MONDALE
Jimmy Carter's Relief Man

GEORGE McGOVERN
Can people remember 12
years back?

Trying to break out of the southern
Sunshine Leagues

Stats: Born January 1, 1922

Minor Leagues: Citadel, University of South Carolina

Electoral Percentages: 1980 70%
1974 70%
1968 62%
1966 51%

(all Senate League)

Quote: Unintelligible due to accent

The veteran shows surprising
strength, centering his energy on
one issue.

Stats: Born June 10, 1914

Minor Leagues: Stanford

Electoral Percentages: 1980 57%
1974 61%
1968 52%

(all in the Senate League)

Quote: ''No Nukes''

Trying to shake off past failures;
always good for a laugh

Stats: Born July 19, 1922

Electoral Percentages: 1980 39.4%
1974 53%
1972 37.5%
1968 59.8%
1962 50.1%

(all races in Senate League except
disastrous year in Presidential)

Minor League: Dakota Wesleyan,
Northwestern

Experienced player looking for
top spot

Stats: Born January 5, 1928

Minor Leagues: University of
Minnesota

Electoral Percentages: 1980 41%
1976 50.1%
1972 51.7%
1966 53.9%

(Last 2 races in VP League; earlier
races in Senate League)

Quote: ''Jimmy who?''